HOW TO BURN A WOMAN

This book comes with a trigger warning for sexual abuse, sexual assault, and descriptions of torture.

Claire Askew was born in 1986 and grew up in the rural Scottish Borders. She holds a PhD in Creative Writing & Contemporary Women's Poetry from the University of Edinburgh. After living in Edinburgh for many years, she is currently based in Carlisle. In 2014 she was runner-up for the inaugural Edwin Morgan Poetry Award for Scottish poets under 30 for an earlier version of her first book-length collection, *This changes things*, which was published by Bloodaxe in 2016. She was shortlisted for the Edwin Morgan Poetry Award for a second time in 2016. *This changes things* was also shortlisted for the Saltire Society First Book of the Year Award 2016, the Seamus Heaney Centre Prize for First Full Collection 2017 and the Michael Murphy Memorial Prize 2017.

She has been a Scottish Book Trust Reading Champion (2016-17), a Jessie Kesson Fellow (2017), and Writer in Residence at the University of Edinburgh (2017-19). Also a novelist, her award-winning Edinburgh-based DI Birch series is published by Hodder & Stoughton. Her second full-length collection, *How to burn a woman*, was published by Bloodaxe in 2021.

CLAIRE ASKEW

How to burn
a woman

BLOODAXE BOOKS

Supported using public funding by
ARTS COUNCIL
ENGLAND

Cover design: Neil Astley & Pamela Robertson-Pearce.

Printed in Great Britain by Bell & Bain Limited, Glasgow, Scotland, on
acid-free paper sourced from mills with FSC chain of custody certification.

For those who've burned, and those who've survived.

CONTENTS

Domonic

This time of year I think of you the most:
springtime, when I'm in love with everything.
Behind the bar you liked on Candlemaker Row

the kirkyard laburnums are budding; come
the summer they'll be yellow Texas hairdos
dropping pods of blossom on the old graves.

I'm amazed that I still observe the days
since you went wherever you went; that
I still want to tell you things. Like:

I look for you in crowds of out-of-towners, and
in spring sometimes there'll be a man who
makes me pause, heart spilling its blooms.

But there was only ever one of you, born
with a misspelled name even Google
corrects. Like: see? I'm searching.

Like: I've learned there are collectors who want
only broken things – porcelain so loved that when
it smashed, the cracks were sealed with gold.

That's how I was broken by your going:
although it was a wrecking, it was also
a making-better. Like: thank you.

Like: what I'd choose to do with you right now
is go to the bar in the big white afternoon, no
one else drinking, the window seat a giftbox

of jewelled light. Laburnum light: amber
in the tall glasses lit up like bulbs. And after,
I could walk away, every break and closure glowing.

Nessie to the unaccompanied minor

Like you, I was unmoored – all my kind
dying – and like you, I'd heard
there may be safe port in this land.
The bottle of the sea loch stoppered.
I watched its neck – through millennia
quick as an eyeblink – narrow, narrow
and I could not move. I was not like you:
couldn't trust my heart, my own
little outboard motor.

But like you, I know what it means
to be hunted: to have nets cast
in your wake, nets barbed
with all the ways they'd like to take
you apart. Out, they send their boats
to find us: out, and out. The search-
lights glitter on the loch like spilt fuel.
As if we don't know boltholes! The art
of disappearing oneself among the rocks.

(They want to find us, but
they also do not.)

Monster to tabloid monster: I'm sorry –
you're starting a loneliness I know
only too much of. This loch
is a big drum I rattle through,
fin over fin, flick over seized old tail sick
of swimming. I'm singing, if
you can bear to be near water
any more. The song goes
alone, alone, alone –

but you know that.
It's the only song you've ever sung.

Playing it cool

When you get to the point
of writing poems about a man,
that's it. Forget your protestations, your
maybe just one drink or *we*
can take it slow. Better to admit
the things you've already let him do
in your imagination's curtained room.
Remember Grant, a walking disaster
of old regret, the way he ashed
his Silk Cut with those nimble hands
so you went home and wrote
his clothes off in ten
bad lines? Yeah – remember
any one of them, these men
with their good teeth, collarbones,
forearms like brown rope mooring
yet another poem, subtext's flotsam
lapping round its parched boards.
Forget your *I just want*
to be alone: the notebook already full
of his brown eyes, mussed hair, smart
lines he fed you and you swallowed – yes,
that's a double entendre – yes,
he's pressed into a sharp suit, he's pulled
you into his overcoat, and how could you *not*
write out the shock of skin against cold silk –
it felt almost wet – and there you go again,
too late – you're hooked, you're sunk,
your cover's blown, and worst,
he knows it now, knows you
couldn't fucking help yourself, you had
to go and write it down.

The flirt

Each instance of it hit me
like a hot rock flung from some
deep reach of space, a place
I'd never been.
I'd never seen such a man
up close, because
women like me aren't usually
allowed. He had a face I knew
would improve with age:
weapons-grade smile, a gaze
that pulled me out of safe
orbit. This can't be happening,
I told myself – each asteroid
more devastating than the last.

I spent decades getting here:
pushing the little craft
of myself out past the markered
reaches, following star
after star. What I made
wasn't beautiful, but God,
it was strong – I'd built
a body I thought I could live in
without burning it down.
He had other ideas, though
I don't know what they were.
I was target practice: the glare
of his attention a smatter
all over my radar.

I fell light-years: can't patch
my trashed rig well enough
to leave. Now the stars
harden in the autumn sky,
but I can't read them.
I'm so weak, I can't even
lift my face, and look up.

Hand of Glory

The Hand of Glory is the dried and pickled hand of a hanged man, combined with a candle made from the fat of the same corpse. The candle, placed in the Hand of Glory and lit, was said to render motionless anyone who took hold of it, or stepped into its light.

Let me stop you right there,
she says, and passes the hangman's candle.
The hand doesn't move in the puce light
unless it is moved – its five digits domed
under the palm – it is huge and pale
as a camel spider. *Sinister*, the murder hand
she cut herself from the swung corpse,
avoiding his gaze, knife scything extremities.
(Executioner stage left,
back turned, palming her coins.)

In pantried lines, the spoils of her gallow
scavenges: you've heard what happens
to hanged men, and her tall jars
measure the evidence. Pickling
pulls the colour out of flesh. The liquids
hold their ghosts' dance of vein,
white skin, fingers, shucked eyes.

She's tried to stay out of town,
hung signs in the trees, made sure
she's well and truly accused. But a few
still come, full-moon-drunk and bent
on crossing the palm of the witch.
This one's tall, well-armed: panic
pink as a birthmark on his paused face.
Wait, she says to them, *hold the light*,
then looks away as the hand
creaks closed on their throats.

She'll work through the night to take
what's good about him – peeling
his skin like a rain-heavy dress, slicing
his nerves. Every creed has a hand
of protection. This one is hers.

Christopher's rules for skimming stones, which are also rules for living

You have to be willing to get
your feet wet, he said – *get close,*
get in its face – as though this
were some tiered stadium
with floodlight and fake grass –
not Rydal on an autumn day,
Chris wading off to ankle-
depth and raising silt, Loughrigg
chucking its bracken net
of reflection onto the lake.

I laced my fingers
with slate chips and skated in
like a woman preparing to drown,
and recall he put his jacket
round me – the sort of slight, kind
thing that happened till the list
of unkind things got written.
Of my ten or so selected stones,
he threw away six: too big.
You shouldn't pick up anything
that doesn't fit in your palm.

I remember those rejects
settling at our white feet –
his a little paler – four
weird fish keeping still
under ripples – his jacket
smelled like cedarwood
from the cabin bed he built
and lived in, all splinters
and two-by-four that clicked
under our moving weight.

Pay attention, he was saying,
showing me his jack-
knifed arm and index finger,
the follow-through that came
after the twist. And the stone
splashed over Rydal's foxed
and silver mirror – seven,
eight, nine – Chris counting in
a song that never began.

He'd use those same deft
hands in anger, and I'd bolt
into a night as unreliable
as lakeland scree. But at Rydal
that day he said to *try,
and keep trying*, and I counted four,
then five and each time
waited to see if he'd smile.
You have to let go lightly, he said –
I wish I'd reminded him.

*You have to get down low and look
at where you want the thing to land,
then put it there*. He closed his fingers
round my wrist, against the pulse.
He put the perfect missile in my hand.

The women who've loved you

I imagine them lined up at the bar
you used to tend, drinking
something called a Greta Garbo: sickly
mustard yellow slush like nightclub doorway
snow, plus sugar and a twist. The first
has got her shit together, just about –
when she says that she's over you, the others
think it might *legit* be true, and hate her
stinking blood. They drink like siblings
at a funeral, like jurors who've condemned a man
to death. They drink to the memory
of their names rolled on your tongue;
the chest they lay their heads upon
in the hot night; the Valentine's Days;
your lentil and potato soup a cure
for anything. When I walk in, they look up
from their neon drinks, their eyes shark-black:
I did this, I'm the reason. They're all wearing
whatever outfit they dolled up in
for your first date – all the jewellery
you ever bought – they're laid down
with trinkets, counting the loose change
of their jewelled rings against the cocktails' stems.
And I'm no different – this is *that* dress,
the polyester floral printed disaster –
who knows what possessed me,
but it worked all right, you peeled it off
that night the way I hoped you would. I threw it out
years back, but here it is again, a little
tight around me now – my boots pinching,
and my wrists, like theirs, all silvered
and cuffed. It takes a minute, but they know
what I've done. I wait, damp handkerchief
balled in my fist, already lifting my puffed
face to catch the barman's eye, and as if

they've discussed it – and all agreed –
they scuff up, pull another stool,
make room for one more.

A Field Journal of Witches

All but the most famous were nameless:
plain women who ended up living alone.
Girls from the next village over –
a cluster of houses at the dirt-track's fork –
and not enough men there to wed them.
So they came up wageless:
forbidden from ploughing or sowing
or even owning much
beyond the black-bellied pot,
the besom's whittled twigs.

They had their wits. When you live
in a shack on the fringe of your known world,
you learn some woodcraft
or you die. So they knew their Jack-by-
the-Hedge from their Robin-
run-in-the-Grass. The shack
attracted vermin, so they kept cats.
The market square
was also where the gallows were,
so they raised crops.

They learned to read the weather
though they couldn't write,
and yes, they understood –
the way the townsfolk couldn't –
that there was no God
when the shelter fell in yet again,
and hunger pitched them
into visions where they flew like birds,
or brought the iron bar of hate down
on the head of every man they'd known.

Wouldn't you welcome your own death?
An end to the bitter winters,

outliving all the women of the village
because you'd never birthed.
Pinned to the stake, or tilted
on the ducking stool, these witches
could pick out the villagers
who'd come to them in secret
through the years with ailments,
begging spells that never worked.

I hope that as the first spark took,
that as they pulled the first cold shock
of water into sunken lungs,
they found their way back to the woods:
the Jack-in-the-Pulpit
and the Dutchman's clogs.
Under the big green cauldron
of trees, the Bruisewort.
Dead men's bells.
Gold moss.

Travel poem

(Friday Harbour, San Juan Islands)

I *Knife fight*

I don't know when I'll see him again.
I want it to be never, because his smile
hurts and he knows it – sits
around all day flipping and catching it
like a blade. But I also want it
to be now: waiting on this bleached porch –
dawn, because I got the time zone wrong –
this island of rusty trucks that
no one's ever heard of, much less
can find. I want him
to pick his way up the sawdust path
towards me, already fingering
the white bone handle –
eyes on the pale flag
of my throat – already planning
the first clean throw.

II *Sac*

My heart's gone quiet
since it happened. It's spun
itself a muffler
of scar tissue, spider-like,
waking up every day
to mend the tears.
On a quiet enough night,
once the tide has laid
the harbour boats on their sides
and stilled their bells,
I can press
an ear to that soft cocoon,
hear it say *you promised*
this wouldn't happen again.

24

III *Instead of him,*

I get a hummingbird. It's August.
Someone's reversing a truck somewhere –
down in the harbour, the first
arriving tanker of the day sounds
its yawn-song, and the echoes
bounce around the archipelago.

I raise my face for the tenth time
in a half-hour, and he's not there –
of course he's not there,
he's never coming, you fucking
idiot, and then – hummingbird.
Dropped like a big hint to be quiet.

Quieter – quiet down. It moves
like it's being thrown: soft rock, bright
fishing lure. No – the fish itself,
its little body liquid, fish-green, scaled.
I don't know what the flowers
it's drinking from are called.

I don't know how it hangs there, everything
in it going ten to the dozen, but it does.
It keeps on and on without rest, like
my heart will, whether it likes it or not,
and I can hear it now, yes – its cautious
what's next? What's next? What's next?

IV *I describe it to Martyna later*

Like a little motor.
Like a helicopter.
Like a hand-held fan –
no, smaller.
Like malachite.
Like labradorite.

Mostly like a fish
with wings –
like –
like –
like the opposite
of a knife.

Devils

for every 'witch' sentenced to death on the grounds
that 'she slept with the devil'

They liked
the pink, misty end
of the day: knew
we'd be sent to fetch
the horses from the pasture,
or we'd be walking away
from the schoolroom,
round the lane's last turn
where the hawthorns knit
into an alleyway
of gibbering birdsong.

They liked the woods,
days when the rain
was fine and the smoke
from the village lay down
among the trees –
or days when the wind
raffled its big cape
and our screams were lifted
and thrown away like the storm-
blown rooks, like all
the garbage of the town.

They were men
who owned things – our father's
land, our parish's
collective souls – always had
some hold over us weak-legged
girls too hungry to run.
Or too afraid: they made us
promise such secrecy,
regaled us with nauseous
threat of what we all,

eventually, got: the courtroom
where we hid our broken
hands and lied
under the hot eyes
of their wives.

We welcomed the fire.
Our cries were cries of joy
as every fingerprint,
shackle-mark, every bite
in our flesh was blistered
clean. They liked
to think they could strip us
off into the places
where men's bodies ruled,
convince us of our own
incurable loneliness.
But we collect our sisters
from the half-world
as their smoke drifts out
and fills the dawn
with its sick, familiar smell.
They were all devils, but
they won't find us in Hell.

The affair

> Someone will pull you from the fire, someone else wrap
> you in flames.
>
> KIM ADDONIZIO

You spend weeks telling yourself
nothing will happen. It feels impossible
as flight: impossible, even as you lay down
the sticks. You walk under the railway bridge
where someone has scrawled *Archie*
the kid is ghosting and think, *impossible*.
You turn from your own thighs in the mirror.
You stalk his ex-girlfriend online
and stack up the coals.

Perhaps it's the season that's doing this:
spring, with its blossoms that fall
for anything, suggestive fingers
of lilac pushed through the hedge.
The badge of his name is pinned
in your buttonhole: a critical
mentionitis case, syllables knocked back
like shots, the world a bar
where no one you know drinks.

Still, impossible, you think, as the room
is unpicked by the first blade of smoke.

I mean. He's built like a deer,
all caramel brown and slim hips,
gaze like a tunnel through woods
where smarter little girls than you
have been lost, wolfed.
Behind you the trees creak
in a wind that stinks
of boiling sap. *I mean*
look at me. He'd never.

29

But something gives. He's wearing this
crisp cotton shirt and all day
you find you're unbuttoning him.
It's going to happen – has
been happening all along.
Look around at the wildfire
you've become: the lilacs,
the railway bridge burning.
Walk over and tear him down.

Giles Corey

d. 1692

Sheriff George Corwin led Corey to a pit... laid him on the ground in the pit, and placed boards on his chest. Six men then lifted heavy stones, placing them one by one, on his stomach and chest. Giles Corey did not cry out, let alone make a plea. [...] Supposedly, just before his death, he cursed Sheriff Corwin and the entire town of Salem.

STACY SCHIFF, *The Witches: Salem*, 1692

Howard Street is a plumb-line: chain link,
asphalt, October, gauze ghosts
tacked to screen doors.
A thrown porch pumpkin smashed
four ways against the fence.
It's midweek, quiet under lime-yellow leaves.

It feels like agreed forgetfulness:
these homes built in the gap of years
and no one left alive who knows
where you were put, beyond *this block,*
somewhere. Beside each painted house,
a truck. Dogs bark. Clouds turn,
and on the park the fairground workers
rev the haunted house awake.

The weight: smell of the donut
fat tanks warming, gasoline on every
well of rain and you could be
anywhere here, your bones flung down
like seed – this place where an uneasy
peace was made. The weight:

this street, the park, the metal racks
of waltzer, dodgem, hotdog stall.
The entire pin-up fairground town.
You bear it all.

Thornfield

Tomorrow he's leaving for good.
You know where he's going, but don't
belong there – couldn't show up
without scaring him. So
it's your last chance. So
what if he's married?
Your heart walks past the shopfront
fifty times without going in.

Your head drives you to the beach.
There's a spitting easterly. It's February,
two degrees, the dunes filled up with snow.
You write his name in the coffee-coloured sand
and the sea licks it up.
Of course he's married. You palm
a good head-stoving rock, then chuck it.
White wave-tops blow sideways out of range.

The town's rinsed out. Somewhere
a clock is wrong – the streetlights on
in daylight. You tell yourself it was just
three times, and the first time doesn't
even count – you don't know
his last name. You wonder
what his wife looks like,
then can't stop.

Night comes without stars.
He locks up the shop for the last time.
The tide is dragged out by its skirts,
your thrown rock dumped in the ebb.
The clock chimes *last-chance,*
last-chance – his smile
like a chipped axe gleaming. Above him,
all the streetlights go out.

Knife

(Moniack Mhor)

You're a half-shut knife, the woman
in the neat scarf says. I'm looking
at the miniature bolts that hold
her natty glasses in the shape
of her face. She's saying it
as an example – *you're a half-
shut knife, that's whit ma
Banff granny used tae say* –
but she's right.

I'm a half-shut knife: not quite
awake, moving in an unscrewed slope
through these rooms, their squares
of blue light. I'm a blunt
edge, folded in the lonely oilcloth
of my bed, not closed but also
never open – zoneless, gutless,
cutting no mustard, splitting no flesh –
in control of essentially nothing.

I'm looking at those
two silver crossheads catching
the light: this woman's eyes
green earths, towed
by their own tiny moons.
She's laughing at me, this wifey –
wise old dove crooning
in Gaelic, appraising me in ways
she knows I understand. *Aye.*

I'm half-shut knife,
all right. I've dropped
from the pocket of my old life –
scratched lines thumbed dim

on my slight blade
right up to the kick –
my loss mourned by no one.
Where is the man whose hand
I could be folded in?

But my new friend is quiet,
her eyes like marbles
in a riveted jar. *Sure*, I say,
a half-shut knife. Closure
is all I'm looking for.

May

It is said that Long Meg and her daughters were a coven of witches who were holding their sabbat, when the Scottish wizard Michael Scot came upon them and turned them to stone. The stones of the circle are said to be uncountable, and that should anyone ever reach the same total twice, the spell would be broken.

BBC CUMBRIA

I was the biggest of us and slow,
second-oldest: long ago
made babysitter, laundress, built
for the heavy lifting,
for a baby on the hip.
I was a shadow thrown
to contrast my sisters' glow.

His was magic I'd never seen –
so green in the ways of men –
his hard science buzzed its puzzles
in my head long after he'd come
and gone. I knew he was lying
all along – finding me in the lane
where he'd told me to be, saying
he wanted me, alone. I knew.
Or I should have known.

The hawthorn was wild that spring,
the hillside ringed: its sweet and lousy
stink on my hands from where
I'd thrashed in the ditch.
I whispered the secrets my mother
had warned me to keep,
my guard peeled back by the glamour
of his naked gaze.

He was afraid, I see that now.
Our brave and homespun craft
enacted by candlelight
and weather, familiars crammed
in the lee as inexplicable rain
maddened the thatch.
We made things happen.
Men have always hated that.

And yet. When I danced,
I danced for him. The blossom-
socked may trees glowed
like our skin in that hot night's moon.
He moved up the hill and I wanted
to scream *he's come for me, I fucking
told you so* to a world that only
ever rolled its one green eye
at my clumsy desires. But I knew.

He was not there for me –
or not only for me.

A spell for the departed

I never visited you,
so I never saw the hospital bed
wedged in the back sitting-room,
its long white bars locked
to stop you dropping off over the side
and sliding on your belly through the house –
its rooms abandoned now,
whitewashed thinly in moonlight –
towards the matchbox, the gas tank, the ladder
or some other disaster;
never saw the litre bottles filled with pills
as big as jelly beans, brown glass
throwing sunlight like the surface
of a dirty pond, safety lids the size
of saucers twisted off in clouds
of powder residue: pill bottles
on the sideboard with the urine flasks
and pads and gauze, the oversized syringes
in their antiseptic plastic packs –
the trappings of your life now –
on the sideboard where my picture
used to sit in its spit-polished frame.
I never came, because I hated you
and this was your house,
so I didn't see, but I hope
it was every bit this bad, and worse.

Sarah Good

d. 1692

> Under the gallows from which she was to hang, Sarah Good
> shot back: 'you are a liar. I am no more witch than you are
> a wizard!' Having lost an inheritance, a home, and a child,
> she added a shrill curse. 'And if you take away my life,' she
> threatened, 'God will give you blood to drink.'
>
> STACY SCHIFF, *The Witches: Salem*, 1692

the girls would call you
old

you were not
old

you'd slept
in a barn that winter

pregnant
your little daughter

wedged half-under
your body for warmth

your baby was born
in the jail and you named her

Mercy
maybe still hopeful in the face of it

there wasn't fuel
to warm the minister's rooms

the milk
froze in its churns

and the sap
in cords of wood

you'd begged
the Christian village for food

for a bed
as the wind rammed its fist

down the Putnams' chimney
clawed glass from the parsonage porch

they dreaded your coming
your hands-out

ragged face
all too well-kennt

they thought
you'd done it

torture and affliction
the winter itself

as if
an itinerant mother would summon

such a thing
as this

the timbers
underpinning

every structure
blizzarded away

old
those girls would call you

one old beggar any village
could live without

one fewer
among many mouths

no   two
because your baby died

that bitter spring
having taken not one

breath
outside

the death-row
cell they held you in

some witch
you were

even her good
good name

not spell
enough

A spell to honour your foremothers

Wait for the half-moon's cleft
guillotine, then pick a side.
Heads it's white,
tails it's black:
these are your chances.

If it is October –
if there is high cloud
writing over the headland
a change in the weather –
so much the better.

Gather your dear things to you,
your essential things:
plate
cat
child
locket
wrap of letters
bread
book
map.
Set them on an anvil and chant
over a white candle.

Roll a taper
from the topmost letter,
and when the twelfth chime
sounds the night's high tide,
set fire
to the letters
to the map
to the bread.
Let the cat scream off into the dark.
Let the child find its own way out.

Let the anvil melt
that whole house down around it.

Do this,
and you will hear them say *okay,*
maybe you get it.
Maybe now you understand.

You can't always get what you want

It might be a good start
if you knew what *what you want*
was. If you stopped trying
to do the right thing: drinking whisky,
buying black underwear, acquiring
a vibrator that leaves you unable
to come under your own steam
for several weeks, and other acts
that scare you even more. Since when
were you the woman swiping lipstick
on the back of her hands
in the department store? Since when
did you take bathroom selfies
in your bra? Just why exactly
are you 3am-ing all over the black
and white diamonds of someone else's
kitchen floor? A clue: it's male
and six foot two and bought you
a drink once – rhymes with *you want
to go somewhere quieter? Want
to get out of here?* Looks like
a lee of green, gauzy shade
on a hot afternoon – answers to
dreamboat, heartbreak, long tall drink
of deadpan smile. Just FYI:
when you think things are going well,
that's a tell-tale sign. But if you pack
your car right now – flashlight, shovel,
cheap wine, Anne Sexton's *Collected*
and the roadmap to your own
potholed heart – you might just make it out
before he rolls back up and kisses you
into the ground. It's possible to be
okay on your own, you know, if you
try sometimes. You might find.

Rodney

(Moniack Mhor)

'I've got no use for romance anymore,'
Rodney says. All week, we've tramped the grit paths
of this place, walked the creaking boards
and talked. Nights, I shake the tiny rocks
from my wet shoes. I'm meant to be writing
poems, Rodney songs. 'I'm on the road,'
he says. 'I'm fifty-two. I got friends.'

This afternoon, Rodney left for Ullapool:
one bag and a tape-patched guitar.
Snow fell around the house in ropes,
March 16th, the stove all smoke, protesting;
crocuses finished off. In Rodney's book,
I read the lines, 'she is the river, the snow
fields, the neon in the rain,' as romantic a poem

as you'll find. But he hasn't lied.
There are nine of us here, in exile
above snowpoles, among drystane, homesick
with north. We think it's true
when we talk, the way I thought at first
how free I'd be, if I could put down romance
too, like a leaf dropped into a well.

The snowfall feathers. *Settle, settle*
clicks the stove. I'd cave before a day
was out, without the love that has me
thinking every hour I'm here of you.
I drive by the headlamp of the good old moon,
each poem the radio dial I turn
for human contact in the dark.

At Ullapool, the stars eke through
the cloud at last, as Rodney
clips the capo on, begins
to sing. You can't tell me he won't
look up, and play for them.

Motorcycle jacket

I couldn't get the boy to kill me, but I wore his jacket for
the longest time.

RICHARD SIKEN

People ask me if the jacket belongs to a man.
I've tried to make it my own, adorn
it with pins, scuff off its corners.

When I can't afford rent I live in this jacket.
But I get it. It may be because it fits me
so well, and I am man-sized.

It's April, month when everything explodes.
The whitebeam trees in the Jubilee Park
fall over themselves like waves.

Their branches crash into the city buses
and the city buses pull bridal trains
of blossom, paintwork, scent.

It might be the Sheffield Wednesday badge
on one lapel, gilt stars on the library ceiling,
it might be the rain.

I've loved a lot of men but none have fit me like this
city with its flat haar, bitter springs,
daffodils crushed like used tissue.

The crowsteps. Sequinned eagle on the back.
This place is my sidecar. Everything here
dove-grey and mauve, my chapter colours.

Could I leave, these choked zips
shiny and jagged as gum-foil,
my pockets filled with ticket stubs?

I'm dialling another man's number, pulled up
at the kerb, every cylinder firing. I'll pull the sleeves
down over my hands, against the cold.

The neighbour of Ursula Kemp
d. 1582

> The said [child] saith that his said mother Ursula Kemp...
> hath four several spirits... and being asked of what colours
> they were, saith that Tittey is like a little grey cat, Tyffin is
> like a white lamb, Pigeon is black like a toad, and Jack is black
> like a cat.
>
> Trial of Ursula Kemp, St Osyth, England, 1582,
> from *The Penguin Book of Witches*

Again, her child is in the field, the smoke
of dawn around him. He's small:
so frail, the sheep don't
raise their heads as he *swicks*
through the grass, sage, knotweed,
nettles belting his legs. He said
in the court that his mother fed
two cats, a toad, and a lamb –
that these were magic.

I wanted to grab him – wanted
to clamp my hands over his sweet,
violet mouth. I'd stood in her kitchen,
seen the spine-bucked lamb she kept
in a box and fed until it died. I'd run
toward her screams the day the fat toad
crawled in over the threshold, parched.
Those cats had dined in my house, too,
though now they've burned.

The sun came warm
into her rooms: her beer sweating
in a stone jug; the white loaf cut
and offered on a blue plate; the range
unmaking its coals. I know
these were bedtime stories told
to the child – and to my

47

unlucky daughters, too. I want
to go outside and gather him –

little pink flint, little bag
of kindling – and bring him
to where I can keep him penned
and bleating, like that ungood lamb.
The men hanged her, and threw away her bones.
Now he's gone, mute and sobbing,
as quickly as he came. I say
a coward's prayer of thanks,
unlock my door, then lock it again.

Hot rod

I don't even know what it is
but I want it, this mod project
hot rod, some boy racer's pride
and joy. I could read by
the reflected gleam of its alloys,
headlight caps, chrome trim
repurposed and shone to pure dazzle
in the Friday sun. I want
someone to come and fire it up,
so I can watch the stunned faces
flick round all along this block. I want
the man who loves this car
to invite me in, holding the door
as I drop through the blue pool
of its roar, my gears kicking up,
every thought a handbrake turn. I want
to peel out from all my mistakes –
his hand on my thigh, whoever
he is – and the cylinders clicking
hot and my heart taking corners
like it's on rails. I want, I want,
I want – face down on the bonnet
like I crossed him wrong, a name
I don't recognise flung
from my lips. I don't even know what it is
but I want it, and we both know what happens
when there's something I want.

Dean

this one has big hands and eyes
                    that change colour
                                        (not

because it sounds good in a poem,
                        they actually do)

tonight
        he's painting a ceiling

(I've never met a man in real life who has his
                    old-fashioned film-star sort of name)

                                        he's a big guy
has to duck under the lightbulb
                        the heat of it on his neck
singeing the hairs he's had buzzed into a soft fade
                        that precious neck
                        those shoulders, endless
                        knotted from the stretch

think of him whistling, stirring the paint with a snub of pencil
                                        it's late
and his eyes turn like spring under their lids

                    outside, the racket of Saturday night
                    buses rattling
                    their spun barrels of change
the paint roller's thick slather still
                        satisfies him

in spite of the day's   long reach

it might be midnight before
                    he steps from the spattery ladder to ask

if I'm still awake
        which I will be
        thinking of those big hands freckled with paint

his ability to enter a room and move it
        from black and white
                    into
                        glorious
                            Technicolor

Coming second

What poem is there
for the day he says
he loves you, but can't
leave her – *sorry,*
it's complicated? I'm tired
of my own heart,
its boring iambs. I wanted
his instead: the unread
stanzas of his body
writing themselves into my bed
as he undressed.
Wanted the heady pulse
of his tongue; shoulder-blades
hung like pages from
his screw-bound spine.

What poem is there
for his wife, who'll likely
never know of me –
never read the line
after line of good verse
I wrote in the air
above our kicked sheets,
then breathed into the white purse
of his ear? It would need
to be a ballad: the done-wrong
heroine showing up at the end
with a sawn-off shotgun.

What poem can tell me
which of us *the other woman*
is? What poem can move
across the memory of his face
and obscure it, like a cloud
blows out the moon?

What poem can drown
his waspy breaths against
my neck – his *sweetheart,*
baby, yes – the memory
wet and sweet as swallowed
liquor, what poem
burns that hotly or that long?
One thing's for sure:
not this one.

Merga Bien

d. 1603

Her pregnancy was considered an aggravating circumstance: she and her husband had no children although they had been married for fourteen years. She was forced to confess that her current pregnancy was the result of intercourse with the Devil.

WIKIPEDIA

Yes, I slept with him. I fell
for his red mouth, the voice that came
out of it. *Girl*, he called me – that one word
like a curl of pale smoke from the woodpile –
the hot coal of his tongue
against my throat. The town dried out
that summer: smell of river bottom,
parched rock, target practice of lightning
on the plateau. I had no other children:
the women flinched away from me
in the dirt square like jackdaws, clattering gossip.
Yet
I was pulled with wanting what
he said he could give. I loved him,
I think. In spite of his disappearances,
rough hands, various flaws.
I didn't believe he could possibly be
who he said he was.

A spell for the rejected

Reject me the way the chainsaw
rejects the oak's claim
to the land. Stand
in the clearing, knee-deep
in the dawn's breath, and rev
yourself into readiness.
Sink your mechanical teeth in
and fell me, then fetch
the red can of paraffin from the truck
you hid in the field. Feel
nothing as the liquid seeps
through my sunk roots fat
as biceps in the fragrant earth. Know
the fox may cry out
at this new scent – the rooks
will escape the canopy via
the dead white space you've left.
Haul everything into the sun and split
and split and split with disgust's
long axe. Bury your cowardice
at the stump. Be the one
to make sure I never grow back.

Mothers of sons

The thing I think about most is who
will care for my no-longer mother-in-law
when she's too thin-skinned for driving,
or cold rain, or walks. She's a while,
but it's coming soon enough
that he and I discussed it, nights,
in bed. His mother's hearing failing
scared him: *this is adulthood*, he said,
and I thought of my some-day care
for this woman I loved because she made
his mind, his two good steady hands.
She only had sons: one overseas, the other
forgetting when Mother's Day was,
standing her up, me at the worktop
rinsing his shirts and cursing
this girl I'd become. His mother
worked through my hazy long-term plan
like an overlocked seam. But now I'm gone.

Perhaps in time there'll be another girl
he'll take to brunch, show off, and hold
in the dark of his mother's sparse
spare room. I think of her, stronger than me
and slim, lifting his mother up out of a chair
in an afternoon filled with low orange sun,
then turning to the kitchen where the medicine
rattles its powdery light. Might I
be in another town by then,
counting change from another
old lady's purse, guiding her down
from a bus, wrists so fragile
in her new wool gloves?
I'll see in her face the frown of a man
I don't yet love, have yet to meet –
and might I steer her home to the house

where he was born, to brew strong tea
as dusk floods under the doors?

And somewhere my own mother,
waiting for my brother's call.
And somewhere my ex forgetting his mum
can't hear: stood on the porch,
one hand on the bell, while a thin rain sugars in,
come down-country from me to him.

Show me again

Show me again
how to take you home

KAREN SOLIE

I've forgotten how to be the woman
I thought I was

show me again

the baltic 2am
tears freezing on my skin
his t-shirt blown against my ribs
his smell
like a bomb-lifted wall
and I said then I'd never be the woman
who did that to someone

show me again

moving away from a past full of men
who should have known better
I said *everything*
on my terms
and meant it at the time

show me again

finding letters my dead
grandfather wrote about me
his *bright, brilliant girl*
cornered by the wash-house wall
sun loud as a trapped cat
and I'm still glad
he died on the cold boards
of pain

show me again

how I said I'd walk out on anyone
who held me
down or stilled me
after then

show me

how I ran here apparently
backwards
in the dark
with no map
landing
in my aunt's kitchen
with one bag and £3.29 in the bank

and she says
again?
and I say
again

Eunice Cole

d. 1680

> ...when she died her body was dragged into a shallow grave
> and buried with a stake driven through it.
>
> KATHERINE HOWE,
> *The Penguin Book of Witches*

I was tired of the cart track
the cattle were driven down – tired of
their spattered white bodies passing
like clouds. The ones
that trailed the pack were whipped with
sticks because that's
what happens to stragglers.
I was tired of living to see
so many grassfed boys
grow like their fathers.

Every year it was February
that almost killed me:
all that winter's patch-up jobs
undone by weather, dead things
in the root store. I was tired
of the cherry in the windy garden,
its hard little buds. I was tired
of the stone in my dark red flesh.

I counted every cobble in the floor of
their jail. I slept on straw
like the whipped grey calf
that never grew right. I dreamed about
the gallows rope holding
its blue teardrop of night.
I was tired of little girls being told
not to come down my road.
They planted me beyond the walls.

In summer, the Lords-and-Ladies
push up their executioners' hoods.
The mushrooms on my choked grave
are dark as boils. Everything
rots with time, even my stake –
my famous stake! Even
my famous heart.

Men

One day a man climbed into my car. A bright day. Ordinary.
It was maybe 2pm, May, the trees all full of themselves. I remember
it was Beaverbank Place, the car awkwardly parked, and I was going
to Lasswade, and I was running late.

The street was cool and blue in the white day.
The key was in, but I hadn't turned it yet.
My tote bag of worksheets, lesson plans, kid scissors, felt pens on
    the passenger seat:
he climbed in and sat on it all, like it wasn't even there.

I think I said, *excuse me, this isn't your car*
before I saw his eyes.

(You always know. When the taunt is coming, when you'll be called
    fat cow,
when it's a snarl, a car horn being blown and the window already
    rolling down,
and they hope that you'll cower. Do you cower, or let the flicked fag
glance off you, did it even happen?

When the men in linen and chinos are going to bray at you – you
    know –
once they've passed: it's like static running between them, the
    decision.
I knew then, too, before he put his face near mine and said
why don't you drive me some place? Anywhere.)

I love men. It's men I call when I'm alone, I'm scared – my keys
    in my hand
with the tips poking out from my fist like I've been shown; when
    I'm done
shouting *get the fuck out of my car* and crying in the road
while other women carry on like they haven't seen –

it's men I call. My dad, my brother, Dom, Leon, Dean.
The police put me in the back of a van. They had to wrestle him
out of the seat, prise off the child lock;
my bag, the vivid pens crushed and leaking.

I knew he wanted to hurt me: wanted it so fiercely
I nearly let him.

A spell for preparing to sleep alone in an unfamiliar house

Open every window. Look out
on the darkening garden, the holly tree
fistfulled with berries, everything
black and lilac, look
at the long grass rising. Listen,
count all the ways you're not alone,
not really: the breeze
spraying aerosol clouds
on the moon's garage wall;

small movements in the hedge;
cluck of gutters; spent stuff blown
into corners, corpses in the patio
door's old webs. Check the shed,
its padlock the colour of pennies, check
under the beds – obviously check
under the beds. Push
a stick elbow-deep
into wardrobes of overcoats,

the rhombus of space
behind each door. Houses warp
and sigh in the night's grip,
a thing you'll learn.
(As a girl, when I'd ask *what
was that noise*, my grandmother
would reply, *something
changing its mind*.) Mind
the lintels and jambs, the in-

between-rooms: each screw
and peg a marker
in the house's map. Remember
its ghosts are lonely, its stove

a mouth sewn shut, gulls
yelling down the flue.
Let out what wants to go.
Be sure whatever stays
has chosen to.

Things men want to hear you say

Mostly, yes. *Yes* – as they press
themselves into you, and yes,
true, sometimes you agree they're
doing okay, but then what else
can you say when they ask
if it was good for you but *yes?* And *yes*,
too, is the only response to the book,
to the meal, to the piece
of jewellery you wouldn't have bought
in a million years: *I loved it, yes.*
Do you want to come
up? Can I call you
back? Do you see what
I mean? Are you listening? *Yes,*
yes, yes – I'm all ears, I'm
all sex, I'm in silk seamed stockings all
the live-long day – my legs
are aching, my girlfriends texting back
and forth: *I know, I know.*
I have to go and find myself a little
piece of something else, though
it may kill me – I'm walking
into its cold and scary
terrain. I hope
there'll be a yellow room, with
one bare bulb, a single hard
and narrow bed, a door that I can close
on *yes, of course, don't worry, I'll*
be fine. The walls of that room
will be built out of *stop*, and *I've*
never liked that you do that to me,
and I will lie down with my own *I'm tired*
and *don't* and *that's not fair* – though
not before I've turned the key
in the lock, put out

the light, and welcomed in the kind
and private dark, whose name
of course – *of course!* – is *no*.

Whisky

(after Kim Addonizio)

Save all your silver to walk up
and ask for it
in your thinnest black dress.
It's kept back – high
above the optics' blank
amber eyes, beyond the ultra-
violet of club light – yet
its flash turns your face
like the quick beam
of a lighthouse.
Pillar of red-hot breath, tall
drink of midnight in the alley
out back, your skirt hiked up
among the kegs. There is no measure,
just two fingers slipped
between your lips,
gold thread stitching delicious
in your blood, and your head
filled with smoke
like a car on fire. Slide
into the black cab it hails
for you – lean back in the dark,
its hand on your thigh.
Your answer will be yes no matter
what's asked, your breath
will be the taste of its shot
bolt in your mouth –
go home with him, it says,
and you're already
on your knees. It's the word
please before the slap
in the face, patterns
in the space behind your eyes,
the pavement's foxtrot whirl.
Go on, it says. Swallow. You know
you're that type of girl.

Watching the red kite trying to fly

(Moniack Mhor)

She knows where she wants to go, but the weather
has other ideas. Sleet in her eyes, she's
lifted on the updraft then shoved
back, her bright tail splayed
like a palm. She lands flat, as a jump-
jet does, a few feet from the same patch
of soil. The wind has taken the valley, and
she can't get over the wall.

                                    You know it all
too well, don't you, wading home
through the shut-up funfair of London,
city where nothing that isn't money
gets off the ground. The clouds
are being rolled south, gathering pace:
you'll turn your face against the squall
as I brace the fire for the night to come,
rinse that same rain out of my hair.
Upcountry. Five hundred miles
not really that far.

                        It's near
enough to miss you, to wish you
a skin-deep wringing at the hands
of this storm. To wish you
were different, less stubborn, or
some other thing. The kite is flung
in a wide ring, and goes down again,
again. It's like that, I think
aloud, against the wuther and creak
of the gale. You're picked up, but
then you fall, and fall, and fall.

Phone sex

We're on the phone and he says *I just came
hard over you*. I'm by the window,
not just clothed but cardiganed – though
he doesn't know – and I realise
the mug of tea in my hand was a mistake:
this conversation's bridge
too far. He's got this voice, see – like treacle
over gravel, like vowels pulled up
at the pit-head and consonants whipped
like the blue sparks under a train. He's
six foot two, six hundred miles away
and I'm weak for his filthy vocabulary.

The day's failed. The light's gone creamy,
smudged – the edges of the glasses dulled
as they dry on the board, my tea
gone cold in its chipped mug – I've been holding it
halfway to my face, listening shocked
and still as though to a break-in at the house
next door. But there's only him saying *oh
baby, fuck* – and I look up, past the scrubbed
windowsill with its pile of books,
past the drying-green poles, their slung line
beaded with pegs. Above the woods, a flank
of rain is gathering, bruise-black: it draws up
in front of the sun like a limousine.

In a minute, I'll watch it take the hill, undo
the road's chaste sash, the fancy up-dos
of the trees all tossed, all loosed. *You're the
best*, he says, in his hot, burned-sugar voice,
and I hear that he's tired from work – perhaps
he wants a cigarette – yes, he'll light one when I've left
and feel the fist of that old need unclenching,
too. I want to say *I love you*, but I don't.

The rain is all around me now, it's swallowing
the houses whole. *It's really going for it
out here* I say, almost without meaning to –
you should see. It's really coming down hard.

Anne Askew

d. 1546

Anne Askew was one of the first women poets to compose in
the English language. She was also the first English woman
to demand a divorce. For her writings and acts of protest
she was tortured and sentenced to death by burning at the
stake.

You lived for a month in the White Tower,
saying nothing in the cross-examination,
saying nothing as the men came in, went out,
as they swung the various instruments
of their work, whistled in the passageways.

It was June, and in the garden by the Tower
where the ladies walked, the honeysuckle pushed
its ragged blooms out of the wall like hands.

They showed you the rack: told you how they'd pop
your hips and shoulders from the sockets, dislocate
your elbows and knees. You didn't speak, but climbed
the device's side, lay your ankles in the straps.

A man once told me, every human being gets
two deaths: the second one's the last time
someone living says or writes your name.

Anne. It's been five hundred and seventy years
since they lifted you down: your secrets still wound
in the cord of your throat, the women whose locations
you withheld awake and listening from their beds.

I am weak, but Anne, I will keep committing your name
as if it's a crime, so the distant children's children of those men
(whose second deaths came long ago)
will know you when you're spoken of.

They'll know that you were twenty-five, that you were told
you would be burned. They'll know that as you waited in your cell,
and though it punished every nerve,
you took up your pen. You wrote it all down.

Men of the rack

(to David Harsent)

Their craft was simple.
They expected it to work
as it always had: ripple
the surface of flesh,
bring the spirit down
like a bird in haar. Every voice
could be drawn out bloody,
won from the day's wait
like a caught fish.
They were experts in men.
That desperation to live
they believed was in everyone.
But the light thinned.
Their ropes cast a rod
on the stone floor.
Her white clothes pooled
where she'd come up shining
into the net and they said
it would be effortless,
the work of an hour.
The idea that she took off her gown
for *them*. The idea there was anything
they could have done – any tool
that would have opened her
beyond those bones
merely hooked from their cups.
Stepping out of that dress
was not surrender, was not
a hand extended to her executioner –
and what striptease ends
with the pole pitched and lit?
She escaped it, the dress.
Just as her legs escaped
from her hips. With broken wrists,

74

she pulled the pins from her hair.
We all leave your world with nothing
but a tight old bundle of pain,
and in our mouths, untold names
of others like us.

Fletcher Mathers

Not much is awake yet.
The train snub-noses into the dawn
and the dawn shrugs. It's not warm.
Polmont, November. Geese.
The gummed rails' murmur.

I tell you about the documentary
I watched, in which
some smart person sought out
Fletcher Mathers, the ScotRail lady.
You don't know her,

under the buffer of your border
river, in London, where everything
is spoken in the dialect *computer*.
But I tell you
one woman gives us this day

our daily bread: incantation
of *Cupar, Leuchars, Dundee,
Arbroath, Montrose.* I know
she recited each calling point –
Crianlarich, where this train will divide –

a magic three times. In a list,
as the penultimate stop,
and each journey's close:
*– and Mallaig. Bathgate,
where this train terminates.*

She said she did it years ago –
Glaswegian actress with a gas bill
to pay – but that travellers still
write letters to tell her of kinks
in the sequence at Dumfries, Tweedbank, Drem.

There's no more dawn at Croy
than there was at Falkirk High. I say
the word *dreich* for you to learn,
but you're sleeping: lean and braced
as though facing a gale-force wind.

But in your weird and moving dream –
cold shuck of glass at your temple
and the tea-trolley's ankle-break whirr –
you'll hear her cast the glamour
of our impending arrival.

One day I'll write her a letter
myself: say I'm thankful
for journeys she's guided me on:
change here for the bus link and services to –
travel in the rear two carriages...

At Glasgow Queen Street you wake,
and it's like she's still guardian angeling –
take all your personal belongings
with you – knowing you're precious
and carefully made.

Take good care, she says, *on the station.*

Listening to Rainymood in Waverley Station

I've been given the word *tenderstem* –
a small poem in itself – and I've got
nothing. I'm sitting in the station listening
to an hour's recorded loop of rain.
Thick rain on a tin roof, and nearby,
thunder. *Tenderstem*
sounds a bit like *thunderstorm*,
a bit like *overspill*, a bit like
Edinburgh, where I am – a bit like
all those things that happen and
won't stop even though you never
asked for them. *Tenderstem*:
your long arm stretched
across the bed after we fought
and couldn't speak, your palm
settling like a storm-downed gull
and it all becoming okay again.
The bent wreck of my heart,
its tender stem of roll-cage, burnt-
out grille, and you, incurable fixer,
sparking up for the weld.
The Helensburgh 3:15 comes in
all slick and fizzy with rain.
The rain streaks down the station's
fretwork roof and I think,
tenderstem. Circuit board. Pentagram.
The terror of giving you everything –
the bent stem of my neck, your tender
ribcage – we should break,
our twin weights pitching out of kilter.
But then, your impossible full-stop
hands, their tender grip
on the rail as you step
from your train and come to me,
through rain like green spring stems
the sky throws and throws.

A spell for obedience

'…and if he told you to jump off a cliff, would you?'

Plateau: beech stand rocked by wind,
timbers creaking like a ship spat up
on the land by some unfathomable mouth.
Two hundred feet down, the surf.
The tide's been out, come back
drunk and lairy, full of wild tales.

I take off my shoes. A gull jumps over
the lip and hangs there crying *dare you,*
dare you in the building haar. I'm here
because you led me – yet again – out
from the harbour of my comfort zone,
beyond the safe and whitewashed wall.

I come to the edge each time and find
it's moved: the ledge a little taller,
shadows black and black under
the overhang. Your hand on the small
of my back like a wet brand. I bend
against the oncoming squall, and feel

the fall in every bone, my spatter
on the plunged beach like a fact
understood. *You want to be a good*
girl, you say, your voice like the high,
hot ray of the headland's lamp.
I tell you, every time, I *do*.

And every time, I jump.

Janet Horne

d. 1727

On one side, the track,
the beck. A shoulder of black
moor. On the other,
the long drop, river
a line in the valley's palm.
The men burn the heather back
in belts, embers spreading
in the dark. My pail
beside the well is always
full, collecting husks
like fish, a pool
the moon drops coins in.

When the smoke lies down
in the yard and the stove
backs up – when the night
outlasts the lamp – I ask
for all the things they say
I have. Hand of a hangman.
Fat of an infant.
A white goose whose flesh
could feed me seven years.
Flight. A buck hare's kick.
For any sickness, a jar
of the cure. Lucifer's ear.

Look. On one side the track,
the beck. A shoulder of black
moor. On the other side,
the long drop. Beyond my door,
their moving lights, imminent
arrival. Foxfire. Smell
of fear. Odd stars.

Big hands

I remember your big felted charcoal wool coat,
boxy as a coffin. You hugged me, wearing it,
and the felt was so thick that it bent in straight lines,
like cardboard does. It was Barbican station,
lemon yellow tiles and a busker somewhere doing
Blister in the Sun. No one in London stays still
that long, but you held on, like you knew
we wouldn't meet again. I didn't want to
let go or take the steps or get on the next
Hammersmith & City heading west.
I could have been your friend.
It would have been hard to settle for,
but I'd have done it.

Library

I could come back here at eighty and it would all be the same
still those blossom lollipops of trees   torn blooms on the tarmac like
    failed tests
still the chained lot where my first ever car drops its garters of rust
still cellophane dust covers on books that spark like the whole place
    might go up
like my heart does   with the door's Halloween creak   when in walks
the brown and long-limbed man   yes
still the brown and long-limbed man   his pale blue shirt
still crisp as an origami fish
still the thick-rimmed specs that his eyelashes kiss
still the smile that sank the ship of my springtime that year   he'll
still be here in the dusty yawn of afternoon sun saying *there she is!*
like all his birthdays have come at once and
still he'll look past me at some other girl and I'll turn
to salt in that ruined car and believe I'll die that night   but won't
still behind me the wind will lift the blossom over the wall
into the air and over the still still still still town

A spell for the unbelieved

Begin the fire
with its weird mise-en-place:
stack of papers,
kindling,
coal in a grubby bucket
damp from the step.
Ripping a *Guardian* up
you'll blanche
at his photograph:
a passing hundred words
of *stands accused* and
is alleged to have.

January's afternoons
are hard enough,
the blue light
never touching down,
one swatch of sun
beyond the roofs.
His wife's
a lawyer.
You never
stood a chance,
in truth.

Do what's safe.
Stay in, keep warm,
and when the itch
to find and kill him
hits its highest
pitch, go
into the yard
and split timber
till you blister.

Twist the paper,
shove his
smirking face
into the grate.

Set it light.
Hope that
something
takes.

How to burn a woman

You will not need kindling.
I think I'll go up quick
as summer timber, my anger
big and dry as a plantation
that dreams of being paper:
the updraft already made
in the canopy, and heading down.

Bring your axe to split me
into parts that you can stack
over the dry leaves, over the coals:
my old coat and my bedding box,
the things given to me by women.
You've heard of spontaneous human
combustion. They say it's fat:
once lit, it flares so white-hot fast
the bones give in.
Make your touch-paper long.

Spread the word that the crowd
who will gather should stand
well back. I am coated
in the accelerant of men:
my craving for their good necks,
their bodies in button-downs
crisp as a new book.

As you douse the embers
I will smell like ground elder
choking the cemetery –
roots looping up
out of dead women's mouths,
a problem thing
you'll never get cleared.

Make the stake thick, the bonds
stiff on my innocent wrists.
Burn me the same way
you burned her: do it
because we took the plain
thoughts from our own heads
into the square, and spoke.

Foreplay

Usually he's quick with the *on your knees* stuff,
but tonight he starts on the hill above my house.
The dark here isn't really, on account of the stars
thick and yellow as gorse, so his loose step
on the path is fast, the sandy gravel
splashing. I hear him stop at the door and pause.

Perhaps his hand is pressed against the wood –
he's shuddering those lungs with one last
bootstrapped pull from the vape that flavours him
cinnamon, clove. He knows I'm up here
in the eaves – my brave little heart unravelled with want –
as he blows a silent howl of smoke into the night's ear.

I'll wait for the latch of his fingers in my hair, for
the quickened things he's promised as long
as I can stand. He's on the stairs now – taking them
slow as a tongue meanders up a spine,
and I'm lying on my plain bed like it's white-
hot coals, my body a hammered blade.

He's on the landing, turning out the light.
He's told me to, so I'll wait, and wait, and wait.

Acknowledgements

I am grateful to the editors of these anthologies where some of these poems previously appeared: *Scotia Extremis: Poems from the Extremes of Scotland's Psyche*; *Uncovered Artistry: Uncovered Voices; 20 Years of Amelia's Magazine*; *The Dangerous Women Project*; and *Lanterne Rouge: The Last*. I am also grateful to the editors of *The Literateur*, *The Selkie*, *Hold My Purse*, and *The Scottish Review of Books*, for giving some of these poems their first home.

'Domonic' placed second in the 2015 Oxford Brookes International Poetry Competition. 'A spell for preparing to sleep alone in an unfamiliar house' was Highly Commended in the 2020 Manchester Cathedral Poetry Competition. 'Listening to Rainymood in Waverley Station' was commissioned by the Paperchain Podcast for the episode themed 'tenderstem', and was broadcast in season two, episode five. The 'A spell for…' poems were performed and recorded as part of *Neptune's Glitter House for Wayward Poets*, Episode 4.

Some of these poems appeared in a draft manuscript which was shortlisted for the 2016 Edwin Morgan Poetry Award.

Many of these poems were written or drafted as part of my month-long 2017 Jessie Kesson Fellowship residency at Moniack Mhor Creative Writing Centre. Still more were written or drafted during a week's Spring Residency at Moniack in March 2019 (where I met the fantastic poet and songwriter Rodney DeCroo, who appears in these pages). I am forever grateful to the staff at Moniack for their generosity, support and friendship.

This collection was begun thanks to an Open Project Fund grant from Creative Scotland.

To the people who supported me through some of what this book describes – especially Leon, Martyna, Stella, Alice, Julies D and G, Sasha, Dean, Natalie, Helen Sedgwick, Marjorie Lotfi Gill, Jona Kottler and Adam Parkin – thank you. Special mention to Al, who understands the mortifying ordeal of being known. Big thanks to the Stevenson/Wyard family for letting me in on local Anne Askew knowledge, and for being totally cool about my weird, witchy, poetic interests. Dom: thank you for absolutely everything.

Thanks and loads of love as always to my mum and dad, and extra special thanks to Nick Askew.

To the men who may recognise themselves in these pages: I did warn you.